Human Doing.

As Perverted. By Primitive Beings.

Bo Kenneth

bokenneth@outlook.de

2019

Förlag; BoD – Books on Demand, Stockholm, Sverige

Tryck; BoD – Books on Demand, Norderstedt, Tyskland

ISBN; 978-91-7463-1609

A Name.

Is a kind of label

An insufficient means. Of identification.

Which typically requires.

A more significant number.

A Name.

May be shared. By others.

By any Tom, Dick or Harry.

Called Tom, Dick or Harry.

My surname.
Was established.
In accordance. With administrative routines.

And my first name.
Was publicly pronounced by a priest.

In a ceremony.
Certifying my existence.
A ceremony. Confirming a principle.
By which. My existence was being certified.
By someone. Who did not know me.
Whose authority. To verify my being.
Was being redefined.
Through the ceremony.

+ + +

Being Human.

Once.

We thought the world was flat.
Some still suspect it is.

A world.

In which we cling. To old dogma.
And always only temporarily unfalsified doctrines.
Confirming the existence. Of a measurable world.
As merely probable.

For most.

The world might still be flat.

Over the centuries.

Very little has really changed.
Since a primitive existential struggle.
Came to dominate all other forms.
Of human coexistence.

Within a primitive reality.

Where problems are mostly caused.
By ignorance.
And obviously outdated ideas. And beliefs.
Still distinguishing a primitive reality.

+ + +

A recently created couple.

Is seen sauntering. Inside a gorgeous garden.

Completely naked.

Like primeval versions. Of Ken and Barbie.

Dressed in matching nothingness.

All such stories.

Include. And accentuate concocted conflicts.
Defined. By the creators.
Of such stories.

Most stories.

Re-present illusions.
As images. And illustrations.
Of an illusory. And imaginary. Human universe.
Sustained by stories.
And conflicts.

Most stories.

Of human coexistence.

Depict the deeds. Of aggressive thugs.

Eliminating enemies.

As evidence.

Of might. And magnificence.

Much creative skill.

Has been employed.

To obscure the obvious obscenities.

Of a primitive tradition.

And primeval struggles.

Much artistic effort.

Is still inspired.

By self-destructive “heroes”.

Struggling to sustain a brutal struggle.

As signs.

Of existential angst.

+ + +

Human beings.

Still believe in gods.

As Omnipotent Beings.

Whose powers.

Have had to be defended.

By primitive beings.

Gods.

Who have demanded. And inspired. Endless death.

And destruction.

And the use.

Of Capital Letters.

\+ + +

Like proverbial primitives.

We are still struggling.
To sustain a ceaseless quest.
Inspired by illusions.
By the "powers".
Of gods.

Without fur.

Or fangs.
We are possibly. Among the most timid species.
Where a common and collective existential angst.
Enhanced by ignorance.
Is still sustained.
By deadly and destructive struggles.
Accentuating. A fatal fallacy.
Among simple and primitive beings.

A tranquil Neolithic era.

Came allegedly to an end.

As aggressive tribes. Cultivating war and weaponry.

Compelled by angry gods.

Attacked and conquered their fellow beings.

To expand their patriarchal powers.

Much like today.

At least in theory.

Modern human beings.

Have to live. With the consequences. Of a cultural crash.

Caused by ceaseless quests.

Commanded by gods.

Assisted by thugs.

Supported by priests.

It is indeed difficult.

To find traces. Of peaceful tribes.

And deities.

Defending feminine and fertile traits.

As seen. In cyclical and life-giving processes.

And forces.

Observable everywhere.

Histories.

Of human doing.

Include and endless string. Of brutal battles.

As the roles. Of self-appointed “kings”.

And “princes”.

Could be violently seized. And brutally protected.

By anyone.

Brutally and violently claiming them.

As “kings”.

Could point to statements.

Sanctioned by gods.

And popes.

Proclaiming royal rights. To rule.

And slaughter anyone. Refusing to submit and surrender.

To claims of royal “power”.

In the absence.

Of bodily brawn.

A promise of “power”. Came to introduce a crucial idea..

Among ignorant and primitive beings.

Aggressive tribes.

Have since sought. To oppress others.

To command and control the lives. Of others.

And each other.

Through careful manipulation. Of “powerful” gods.

As a precondition.

For killing and eliminating others.

And each other.

+ + +

We are indeed.

Being punished.

In accordance. With primitive principles.

Preserved through centuries. Of ceaseless struggles.

Seen as natural.

And preordained.

A painful age.

Of countless wars. And common horror.

Constitutes a brutal background.

For primitive beings.

Blindly and brainlessly struggling.

To repress each other. And others.

In an effort. To “ascend”.

From a man-made Hell.

Still immersed.

In an existential soup.

We still struggle. To sustain the pain.

And suffering.

Distinguishing a long and bloody era.

Of endless rivalries.

Among tribal “princes”.

We seem ill fit.

To live alone.

As timid and ignorant beings.

Deeply dependent on others. And each other.

Still seeking to submit. And surrender.

To fellow beings.

Equally dependent on others.

An existential dilemma.

Involves a fatal lack. Of comprehension.

As to common coexistence.

As primitive beings.

In need of ruthless "rulers".

Ceaselessly struggling. To preserve their "power".

And paranoia.

Up through the ages.

Most aspects. Of human coexistence.
Have been seen. As areas of rivalry.
And reciprocal exploitation.
Inspired. By brutal “rulers”.
And Superhuman Beings.

A proverbial Fall.

Occurred.
When angst and ignorance.
Came to govern. And dominate. A subsequent decent.
Into a man-made Hell.
Sustained by ceaseless struggles.
To “survive”.

Motivated.

By angst and ignorance.

We have adopted. A kind of parasitic logic.

Which includes. A vital element of violence.

Explicitly expressed.

By anxious and aggressive thugs.

Battling to eliminate enemies.

And alleviate their angst.

A parasitic practice.

Sustained by beings.

Struggling to sustain a social hierarchy.

Through work. War. And worship.

Motivated and maintained.

By the power. Of angst.

The Power. Of Angst.

Once described.

As *The Naked Ape.*

Still primitive human beings. May similarly be seen.

As anxious animals.

Blessed.

And cursed.

With a vivid imagination.

Coupled. With a crucial lack. Of critical reflection.

"Man" maintains a human universe.

Broadly governed by gods.

Significantly.

Most gods have evolved.

As angry and aggressive deities.

Obsessively.

Demanding absolute and unconditional submission.

And surrender.

To curious commands.

Pivotal.

To centuries. Of ceaseless struggles.
Gods have been seen. As crucial.
To the perception. And appreciation. Of "power".
As possibly the most deceptive and destructive idea.
Distinguishing human Histories.

Where

The prospect of divine might.
Is still seen. To substantiate the Histories of "politics"
As accounts.
Of ceaseless quests.
For "power".

Where all ambitious "rulers".

Have had to maintain a crucial relationship.
With commonly acknowledged gods.

While all ambitious “rulers”.

Have needed priests. And popes.

To sanction the status.

As well as the might. And right.

Of “rulers”.

And gods.

Similar.

To ideas of divine might.

Notions of "power" are based on angst.

As inverse and complementary aspects.

Of broadly the same mental and emotional "energies".

Where "power".

Points to "forces". Prompted by what we fear.

While struggles.

For "power".

Will more than much else. Seem instrumental.

In preserving forms of social and existential angst.

Sustaining such struggles.

At the core.

Of a human universe.

A common and collective angst. Will seem to rest.

On a conscious and unconscious awareness.

Of “absence”.

Enhanced. By efforts. To remain “present”.

Effectively.

Sustaining forms of common and collective angst.

A ceaseless struggle.

For “presence”. And “power”.

Will frequently seem to increase. The prospect.

And probability.

Of “absence”. And death.

Stimulating.

And sustaining. A ceaseless struggle.
The presence. Of "power".
Is inherently ephemeral.
As intrinsically linked to an always present prospect.
Of "absence".

Accentuated.

By "absence".
By an always present prospect.
Of poverty and privation.
The presence. Of "power".
Has to be ceaselessly renewed.
By struggles. Spurred and urged.
By the "power". Of angst.

+ + +

The “power”.

Of angst.

Expressed. As a ceaseless quest.

For “presence”. And “power”.

Sustained. By angst.

The “power”.

Of angst.

Sustaining. A common and collective struggle.

For “survival”.

As a promise. Of “presence”.

A promise.

Of "power".

Preserves. And supports.

An aggressive and destructive struggle.

Effectively enhancing the angst.

As an endless effort. Aimed at alleviating the angst.

A promise.

Of "power".

Will hence appear. As illusory.

And as inherently irrational.

As sustaining a common form.

Of self-deception.

Customarily involving work, war and worship.

Dependent.

On work, war and worship.

A promise of "power" relies on forms of submission.

Where John Kenneth Galbraith distinguishes.

Between;

"Condign, compensatory and conditioned power".

Intended.

To "win submission".

"Condign power" involves threats of violence.

Whereas "compensatory power" rests on promises.

Of "affirmative reward".

"Conditioned power".

Is seen as based on belief.

As "the fact of submission".

Is not invariably or habitually recognized.

A promise.

Of “power”.

Is hence linked to the presence of others.

And to what Max Weber refers to.

As “imposing one’s will upon the behaviour”.

Of others.

A substantial share.

Of the angst tormenting common human beings.
May hence be seen. As emanating.
From the efforts of others.
Seeking to alleviate their angst.
Through the efforts.
Of others.

Struggling.

To compensate.
For lack of fur and fangs.
Timid human beings. Have habitually sought.
The might. Of the many.

Including.

An always present threat of violence.

Backed by armaments and weaponry.

The “power” of the flock.

Is essentially expressed. As a certain capacity.

To cause pain. And suffering.

Death. And destruction.

Significantly.

The “powers”. Of “rulers”.

Invariably depend on flocks.

Whether as “armies”. Of underlings.

Or as the might. Of the “masses”.

Flocks.

Seen as embodiments. Of strength.
Crucially contributing.
To otherwise elusive and illusory notions.
Of “power”.

Flocks.

Seen as crucial. And indispensable.
To any “ruler”.
Seeking to summon. And assemble.
The most momentous. And numerous.
Flocks.

In so far.

As timid human beings.
Fear the “absence”. Of “rulers”.
All “rulers” are seeking the support. And security.
Offered by flocks.
By a common fear. Of flocks.
Of the “absence”.
Of flocks.

Where flocks.

In order to appear as proper flocks.
Are seeking. And struggling.
To be “ruled”
By “rulers”.

"Rulers".

Idealized as "leaders".
As principal protagonists.
Portrayed in stories. And Histories.
Of aggressive and destructive deception.
Maintained by angst.

"Rulers".

As "leaders".
Personifying pomp and pomposity.
As signs. Of "presence" and "power".
And as attempts.
To belittle and humiliate timid beings.
As underlings.

"Leaders".

Seen as essential.
To claims of common and collective submission.
And surrender.
To work, war and worship.
Aimed at maintaining. And enhancing.
A ceaseless financial flow.

Modern forms.

Of common coexistence.

Are fundamentally maintained.

By millions. And billions. Of underlings.

Compelled. And coerced.

To enhance. And expand. A ceaseless quest.

Of acquisition.

And accumulation.

A ceaseless quest.

Sustained.

By a collective competitive and destructive struggle.

Motivated.

By an all-pervasive and persuasive promise.

Of monetary might.

Monetary might.

Is essentially based on angst.

On an always present prospect.

Of social and existential "absence".

Endorsed.

By ideas. Of divine might.
A transient and elusive promise.
Of monetary might.
Is conditioned by common and collective submission.
And surrender.
To a ceaseless quest. Of acquisition and accumulation.
Further spurred.
By monetary relativity.

Where millions.

And billions. Of timid beings.
Perverted by angst. And irrational beliefs.
Actively and aggressively contribute.
To common and collective oppression.
And repression.

The “presence”.

Of monetary “power”. Is inherently illusory.
And essentially sustained.
Through the struggles. Of others.
Essentially employed.
To acquire assets.
Held by others.

Typically.

And dependably.
An aggressive and destructive quest.
For “presence”. And “power”.
Will invariably accentuate a certain awareness.
As to social and existential “absence”.
And angst.

Sustained.

And substantiated. By angst.
The transient “presence”. Of monetary “power”
May at most.
Momentarily and temporarily. Alleviate the angst.
And obscure an omnipresent prospect.
Of “absence”.

A ceaseless quest.

For “money”. And “power”.
Has consistently corrupted centuries.
Of common coexistence.

Most wars.

Are fought. For “money”.
And “power”.
As illusory ideas.
Preserved. And enhanced.
By countless wars.
And centuries. Of ceaseless efforts.
Sustained. By angst.

Parasitics.

In spite.

Of every good intention.

No one.

Of the millions. And billions.

Sharing a human universe.

Is born free.

Or equal.

Young.

Human beings.
Are told to be good.
And taught. To compete.
Educated. And encouraged
To surrender themselves.
To a ceaseless competitive frenzy.

Most forms.

Of common human coexistence.

Are conditioned.

By an aggressive competitive struggle.

To acquire. And accumulate.

"Assets". And "profits".

Seen as vital.

To the struggle.

Where some struggle.

To enhance their struggles.

Through the struggles.

Of others.

While most struggle.

To enhance others.

A fundamentally.

Antisocial struggle.

Is thus seen.

As crucial.

To social and existential coexistence.

Referred to.

As “business”. And “trade”.

A range of parasitic plots. And ploys.

Are employed.

As endless efforts. To acquire “assets”.

From others.

Predominantly. Through the efforts,

Of others.

"Business".

And "trade".

As forms of fraud.

Maintained by greed.

And motivated. By anything.

Remotely offering.

A promise. Of "profit".

"Business".

And "trade".

As parasitic practices.

Involving. And assuming. The work of others.

Pushing and peddling anything.

Having to be pushed and peddled.

To appear as "goods".

And "services".

Parasitic practices.

Depend on deceit.

On acquisition. And accumulation.

Far beyond.

Any rational or reasonable purpose.

Or concern.

As to social or existential consequences.

Parasitic practices.

Preserved.

As pursuits of “profits”. And “prosperity”.

Made manifest. As “property”.

And “possessions”.

"Possessions".

And "prosperity".

As signs. And signals.

Of infinite greed.

Typically visualized.

As shows of affluence. And opulence.

As things and tokens.

Seen as "costly".

Affluence.

And opulence.

Amassed as evidence. Of aggression.

And addiction.

Paraded.

As "ambition".

A ceaseless.

Parasitic quest.

Includes “commercial” activities.

Involving “teams”. Or flocks.

Called “companies”.

And “corporations”.

Seen as statements.

Of “free will”.

Portrayed. As offering prospects.

Of “freedom”.

Through daily labour.

A ceaseless.

"Commercial" quest.

Involves work.

And war.

As fundamentally destructive forms.

Of common coexistence.

Most forms.

Of work. And war.

Present and provide a threat.

A global hazard.

Which would otherwise be seen.

As epidemic.

Where work.

Will seem to cause.

More death. And destruction.

Than most wars.

Most forms.

Of work and war.

Are essentially irrational.

And detrimental.

To all involved.

To the physical.

And mental health.

Of millions. And billions.

Facing costs. And consequences.

Far exceeding.

Any financial yield.

Most.

Of the misery. And savagery.

Tormenting millions. And billions.

Are caused.

By ceaseless struggles.

Seen as essential. To sustain the lives.

Of millions. And billions.

The “energy”.

Propelling a ceaseless struggle.
Is rarely recognized as angst.
Where infinite greed.
Will seem motivated. And maintained.
By more.
Than mere desire.

Whereas desire.

May seem motivated.
By the absence. Of presence.
Angst. Is aroused.
By the presence. Of absence.

One cannot.

Merely point.

To the presence of desires.

To comprehend. The violence. And savagery.

Distinguishing.

A parasitic frenzy.

Decisively dependent.

On “others”.

A parasitic quest involves sustaining. And constraining.

The struggles. Of “others”.

While minimizing. The costs.

Of oppressing others.

As a kind.

Of ongoing war.

A parasitic frenzy.

Persistently involves. The efforts.

Of almost all “others”.

Frequently including old women.

And small children.

Where angst.

And aggression.

Accentuate the fear.

And paranoia.

Through which most “others”.

May be seen.

As rivals.

Promoting.

Promises of “presence”.
Parasitic struggles are reliably enhanced.
By always present prospects.
Of poverty. And social “absence”.
Including. The “absence”.
Of daily labour.

Endorsed.

By “politics”.
The plot and ploys of parasitics.
Include the “art”. And “science”.
Of social and existential fraud.

Promoted.

And protected.

By the “art”. Of pushing and peddling fictitious ideas.

A parasitic frenzy defines. And depends on.

“Commercial” deceit.

As a deeply destructive and deceptive struggle.

Based on infinite greed.

Among those “possessed”.

By “possessions”.

Where a global.

Parasitic quest.

Will seem to re-define. And depend on.

Common ignorance.

And forms of common self-deception.

Essential. To the struggle.

Based.

On belief.

And collective “blindness”.

The integrated “politics” of parasitics.

Is further enhanced.

By social and existential hierarchies.

Seen as natural. And rational.

And essential. To common notions.

Of social “presence”.

And “difference”.

Infinite Inferiority.

Almost all stories.

And Histories.

Depicting human being. And doing.

May be seen as simplified. And standardized accounts.

Of "heroes".

Struggling. To sustain the roles.

Of "heroes".

Almost all.

Such stories.

May be seen as instances. And illustrations.

Of narrative deception.

And distortion.

Typically.

Such stories. And Histories.

Are sustained. By fictitious "heroes".

Struggling.

To sustain illusions.

Some stories.

Are offered. As Histories.

As fictitious accounts.

Seen as factual.

Historical accounts.

Are frequently fallacious portrayals.

Of "rulers".

Idealized as "heroes".

And depicted for the education.

And enlightenment.

Of lesser beings.

As samples.

Of deception.

Historical accounts. Re-present and reiterate illusions.

And fictitious ideas.

Preserved. And promoted.

As preconditions.

For such stories.

Always constructed.
And sometimes contrived.
Most stories. And Histories.
Include a kind of logic.
Which at the same time commands.
And constrains.
The telling.

Repeatedly redefined.
Through the tale.
This kind of logic.
Demands. And depends on.
Solving concocted conflicts.
Conditioned by countless stories.

Almost all such stories.
Include a “hero”.
A conflict. And a destructive struggle.
In which “heroes” occasionally perish.

The role.

Of the “hero”.

Resembles that. Of an ancient scapegoat.

The one chosen to surrender and sacrifice his life.

For the lives of the many.

The ones.

Once worshipped and glorified as “kings”.

To enhance their “sacrificial values”.

Prior to being offered.

To mollify gods.

A practice.

Later reversed.

By Historical “heroes”. And “kings”.

Assuming their roles.

To enhance their struggles.

At the expense of the many.

As fictitious figures.

“Kings” and “heroes” are persistently portrayed.

As principal protagonists.

Personifying primitive ideals.

For timid and primitive beings.

In a ceaseless.

Vicious circle.

Timid and ignorant beings.

Are seen to need “heroes”. And “kings”.

Who in turn need ignorant and timid beings.

To be seen. As “heroes”.

And “kings”.

As imaginary characters.

"Rulers" are frequently seen.
As "heroes".
Glorified and celebrated.
As conspicuously visible.
And required.
To appear as "powerful".

As imaginary characters.

"Rulers".
Are subsequently "sacrificed".
When their "powers" appear to fail.
And a new "ruler" is needed.
To sustain the fiction.

Similar.
To previous “kings”.
Modern “rulers” are still needed.
As figureheads. And “fall guys”.
For flocks. Of the fatal few.
Vitally dependent on “rulers”.
To “empower” and endorse the fatal few.

Flocks.
Of “nobles”. Still need “kings”.
And “heads” of states.
To justify. And glorify.
A detrimental. And antisocial parasitic struggle.
As god-given.
And beneficial to all.

Assumed.
As allies.
Flocks of “nobles” are still needed.
To boost and back the “ruler”.
Required.
To protect and preserve the “power”.
And “properties”
Of the fatal few.

Evolved.

Through struggling. To sustain the struggles.
Of others.
The fatal few will seem.
To confirm a common claim.
As to “the survival of the misfits”.

Mainly motivated.

By greed.
The fatal few may be seen.
As influenced. And inspired.
By centuries. Of parasitics.
Sustained by fear. Of poverty.
And inferiority.

Obsessed.

With accumulating “assets”
Acquired. From others.
The fatal few persistently support.
A ceaseless parasitic struggle.
Sustained. By others.

Assisted.

By “politics”.

The logic of parasitics. Includes violence.

And war.

As means. Of eliminating enemies.

And rivals.

At times. To the extent.

Of extinguishing all “others”.

Where most wars.

Will appear.

As excessive expressions. Of destructive fears.

Among anxious and aggressive beings.

Obsessed with shows of “power”.

And supremacy.

Employed. To quell.

Any hint. Of inferiority.

Between.

The wars.

A common and collective angst.

Is maintained.

As a precondition. For a parasitic struggle.

Sustained by violence.

And infinite inferiority.

From.

A fundamental fear.

Of poverty. And inferiority.

The fatal few. Are propelled.

By greed.

Seen. To offer “freedom”.

And “prosperity”.

To almost all

Sustained.

By ceaseless destructive struggles.

Infinite greed. Is commonly seen.

As crucial. To overcome the problems.

Caused. By ceaseless destructive struggles.

Aroused.

By angst. And inferiority.
Infinite greed.
Includes aspects of irrationality.
Bordering. On insanity.
Preserved. By self-deception.

Greed.

Motivated. And maintained.
By fiction.
By stories. And Histories.
As statements. Of addiction.
And self-deception.

Greed.

Compelling practices.
Of self-destruction.
Conditioned. By "politics".
And "governed".
By parasitics.

Greed.

Among crafty and cunning beings.
Seeing crises. And crashes.
As occasions. To crush rivals.
While amassing more.
For less.

Greed.

Among beings.
Perverted.
By preserving and antisocial "heap".
Sustained. By irrationality.
As a detrimental antisocial hierarchy.
Which would crumble.
And collapse.
In the absence.
Of primitive parasitic fools.

Rather.

Than caused. By eating apples.
Human corruption. And perversion.
Will appear. As intimately linked.
To timid and primitive beings.
Seeking. To savour. The fruits.
Of fraud.

Feudal Fools.

In a post-postmodern.
And possibly pre-diluvian world.
Wars. Only occasionally rival work.
As common forms.
Of collective coexistence.

Wars.
Are mostly fought.
When work is seen as an insufficient means.
Of acquisition.
And accumulation.

Work.
Is occasionally intensified. And expanded.
As war.
As an extreme expression.
Of aggressive. An destructive.
Addiction.

As a kind.

Of distinctly destructive work.
Wars are predominantly fought.
To preserve and protect the “politics”.
Of parasitics.

Wars.

Are mostly fought abroad
To conquer others
To acquire assets. Required.
To conquer others.

Significantly.

Wars are frequently fought.
To appear impressive. And persuasive.
As attempts. To vindicate. And validate.
The “power”. Of angst.
And inferiority.

Wars.

Are always fought.
By flocks.
Of timid beings
Seen as “soldiers”. And symbols.
Of subservience.
And submission.

Timid beings.

Required.
To risk and ruin their lives.
To “survive”.

Timid beings.

Motivated. By angst.
While struggling to be seen as “heroes”.
In accordance. With ideas. And illusions.
Seen as crucial.
To common coexistence.

Inherently irrational.

And detrimental.

Wars. And work. Assume and sustain.

A certain mental blindness.

As sacrificial rituals.

Of common and collective self-deception.

And beliefs.

+ + +

Beliefs.

Have almost always. Been seen.

To sanction and support.

Almost all wars.

Beliefs.

Are comparable.

To delusions.

As subjectively dependent. And collectively conditioned.

Fictitious convictions.

Beliefs.

Are often “officially” approved.

And consolidated.

As a common and collective tradition.

Of often conflicting convictions.

Sustained.

By education.

Centuries.

Of aggressive and destructive struggles.

Have persistently. Been inspired.

By primitive beliefs.

Comparable.

To "life-lies"

Beliefs contribute to sustain a ceaseless quest.

For "survival".

Which has consistently caused more death.

And destruction.

Than anything else.

As both cause.

And effect.

A common "life-lie". Embraces a collective process.

Of self-deception.

Through including. And depending on.

A detrimental lack.

Of critical reflection.

A “life-lie”.

Is seen. By Herman Tønnessen.
As affording. A kind of “euthanasia”.
Among timid and primitive beings.
Whose abysmal angst. Of death and “nothingness”.
Is conspicuously visible. In pyramids.
And “cycloptic” cathedrals.

+ + +

In spite of.

Recurrent crises. And crashes.

A parasitic struggle is still seen.

As natural.

And rational.

To almost all.

A parasitic struggle.

Is still seen to offer promises of “presence”.

As opposed to poverty.

And social destitution.

Blinded.

By angst and ignorance.

And shining symbols. Of social status.

Timid being still compete.

To surrender themselves

To the struggles. Sustaining and substantiating.

Feudalism.

Powered.

By machinery.

And millions. Of feudal fools.

The "politics". Of parasitics.

Embraces a range of endeavours.

Aimed at appropriating "assets".

From millions.

Of feudal fools.

Fairly stable.

Feudal "states".

Are persistently preserved.

By self-preserving serfs.

Cheered as "customers".

Compelled. And all but coerced.

To "consume".

Feudal “states”.

Are mainly maintained. And financed.
By millions of feudal fools.
Struggling. To spend and squander.
To meet the needs.
Of governments.
And corporations.

Mocked.

As “masses”.
Millions of feudal fools.
Struggle to serve. And support.
The frenzies. And addictions.
Of comparatively few.

Timid.

And naïve.
Feudal fools see themselves as “citizens”.
Inspired. By promises of “ownership”.
As signs of freedom.
Sustained by debt.

Feudal fools.
Are easily deceived.
As “voters”.
Voluntarily “electing” to be “ruled”.
And subdued.

Further.
To centuries of suffering.
An antisocial feudal “state”. Is still sustained.
By feudal fools.
As salaried serfs.
Struggling to submit. And surrender.
To feudal “rulers”.
Seen as “leaders”.

Compelled.
By angst and self-deception.
Feudal fools.
As fatal fools.
Are still struggling. After centuries.
Of self-destruction.

Backed.

And bolstered.

By the “politics” of parasitics.

Feudal “states” are primarily preserved.

By primitive beings.

Struggling. To be “governed”.

And “ruled”.

By primitive beings.

Still dependent.

On work. And war.

Feudal “states” are truly “ruled”.

By pursuits. Of “profits”.

Commanding millions.

Of feudal fools.

Equally inspired.

By centuries of suffering. And self-deception.

Ceaselessly sustained.

By pursuits. Of “profits”.

Further.

    To a long tradition.
    Feudal “states”. Decisively depend.
    On flocks. Of brutal fools.

As bestial.

    And brainless beings.
    Struggling to oppress others.
    And each other
    To preserve. And protect. A long tradition.
    Of feudalism.

Subsequent.

To more modern ideas. And ideals.
Feudal "states" are ideally maintained.
By less messy means. Of manipulation.
Adapted.
To preserve a pacified population.
Of productive fools.

In spite of.

More modern ideas. And ideals.
Feudal fools actively accept. And acknowledge.
Feudal "rulers".
As principal and "leading" beings.
Possibly "empowered".
By gods.
And flocks.
Of feudal fools.

In the absence.

Of feudal fools.

Feudal “states” would crumble.

Disintegrate. And disappear.

Leaving feudal “rulers”. To appear.

As feudal fools.

Fearful.

Of freedom.

And actively maintaining. The comfort.

Of ignorance.

Feudal fools will seem unwilling. To comprehend.

And end.

A detrimental feudal struggle.

Fatal Fiction.

One is told.

That truth.
Is the first victim.
Of all wars.
Which is not quite true.

Truths.

Are inherently illusory.
As some truisms. Are merely well preserved.
And persistent.
Fictions.
Protected. And promoted.
Through processes. And practices.
Which include war.

Most wars.
Are motivated.
By fictitious and fallacious.
Truths.

Through.
Work, war and worship.
We have aggressively maintained.
A fictitious realm.

An all-embracing network.
Of fictitious ideas. And ideals.
Maintained by stories.
And Histories.
Of work, war and worship.

Among.

“Man’s” most persistent truths.
Are axioms. Of human superiority.
And sanctity.
Illustrating the nature.
Of truth.

Histories.

Of human supremacy.
Are regularly retold.
As accounts. Of gods. And human “heroes”
Illustrating. Creative storytelling
Frequently claimed.
To be true.

Blinded.

By the presence. Of gods.
And “heroes”.
We have maintained a narrative tradition.
Conditioned. By fictitious configurations.
Rather.
Than intelligent reflection.

Rather.

Than address. And explore.
An irrational "reality".
Timid human beings. Have persistently.
And violently
Defended fictitious dogma. And doctrines.
As pivotal.
To work, war and worship.

Some.

Of the most outrageous atrocities.
Recorded.
By human Histories.
Have been perpetuated. In defence.
Of Christian fiction.

In the course.

Of Christian witch-hunts. And Inquisitions.

Conquests. And Crusades.

Jens Bjørneboe conservatively estimates.

That at least three hundred million people.

Including babies and old women.

Have been slain and slaughtered.

Boiled in oil.

And burnt ant the stake.

At the outset.

Of another millennium.
Significantly calculated. In accordance.
With Christian fiction.
Common forms of self-deception.
Still need to be sustained. And redefined.
Through common and collective surrender.
And submission.
To ritualistic practices.
Including work, war and worship.

\+ + +

A human universe.

Is essentially. A mental realm.
Recognized. Or rather re-cognized.
Within the networks. Of the human mind.
Where the mind.
Is the medium.
Of human being.

A human universe.

May be seen.
As an endlessly emerging realm.
Shaped. And simplified.
By primitive beings.
As a primitive. And destructive "reality".
In which the mind.
Is severed. From the body.

A human universe.

Embraces processes. And practices.
Motivated. And maintained.
By contradictory convictions.
And irrational beliefs
Comparable. To delusions.

A human universe.

Is sustained.
By processes.
Of common and collective self-deception.
Effectively masking.
The transient and transparent nature.
Of an always incomplete.
And insufficiently understood.
Human universe.

Struggling.

To sustain. A fictitious realm.
We simultaneously redefine.
An irrational. Illusory.
And deeply deceptive.
Existential "reality".

An existential universe.

Of absence.
Which effectively enhances.
A common and collective existential angst.
Sustained.
By the absence. Of common comprehension.
As to the dynamic nature.
Of nature.

If anything.
Histories of bloodshed.
And destruction.
Will illustrate. A detrimental lack.
Of intelligent reflection.

Illustrating.
The absence.
Of real "heroes".
And Superhuman Beings.
Such stories. And Histories.
Highlight. And underline.
Still primitive and primeval forms.
Of so-called coexistence.

Hardly verifying claims.
As to human supremacy.
"Historical" accounts may rather seem.
To offer overwhelming "evidence".
As to ceaseless suffering.
And devastation.
Still distinguishing
A human "reality".

The term.

“Realty”.

Will seem to suggest.

A solid and objective background

For a human drama.

Where we as actors. As well as spectators.

Maintain the play.

Playing roles. Predominantly predefined.

By the play.

Which was never meant.

To be a tragedy.

We are easily deceived.

Preferring. The comfort. Of illusions.
To the fruits. Of knowledge.
Where fictitious ideas.
Are remarkable resistant.
To attempts.
At rational. And radical. Reflection.

Endorsed.

By worship.
And assisted. By angst and ignorance.
Work. And war. May be seen.
As collective. And aggressive forms.
Of self-deception.

We have.

Perhaps.

Never truly tried.

To understand. And comprehend.

The processes. And principles.

Defining. And maintaining.

An illusory “reality”.

Instead.

In accordance. With studies.

Of “holy scriptures”.

Scientific explorations. Are customarily constrained.

By rigorous requirements.

As to being “scientific”.

Aimed. At verifying “truth”.

In school.

We are educated. In accordance.

With an integrated network.

Of fictitious configurations.

As a precondition. For an all-embracing practice.

Of acquisition and accumulation.

As processes. Of parasitic deception.

And self-deception.

We still believe.

In gods.
And “heroes”.
As confirmed. By countless stories.
And by the absence. Of stories.
Without “heroes”.
Or gods.

Taught.

And trained.
In accordance. With practices and processes.
Of common self-deception.
We struggle. To sustain. A fictitious realm.
In which gods. And imaginary “heroes”.
Still appear. As embodiments.
Of angst. And ignorance.